History *of* Britain

Trade and Transport

Andrew Langley

Illustrated by M. Bergin, J. Field, J. James

HISTORY OF BRITAIN – TRADE AND TRANSPORT
was produced for Heinemann Library
by Lionheart Books, London.

Editor: Lionel Bender
Designer: Ben White
Editorial Assistant: Madeleine Samuel
Picture Researcher: Jennie Karrach
Media Conversion and Typesetting: MW Graphics
Educational Consultant: Jane Shuter
Editorial Advisors: Andrew Farrow, Paul Shuter

Production Controller: Anita Aggarwal
Editorial Manager: Andrew Farrow

First published in Great Britain in 1998 by
Heinemann Library, a division of Reed
Educational and Professional Publishing Limited,
Halley Court, Jordan Hill, Oxford OX2 8EJ.

MADRID ATHENS
FLORENCE PRAGUE WARSAW
PORTSMOUTH NH CHICAGO SAO PAULO MEXICO
SINGAPORE TOKYO MELBOURNE AUCKLAND
IBADAN GABORONE JOHANNESBURG KAMPALA NAIROBI

ISBN 0431 057265 Cased   ISBN 0431 057303 Paperback

British Library Cataloguing-in-Publication Data.
A catalogue record for this book is available
from the British Library.

Printed in Hong Kong

Acknowledgements
Picture credits
Pages 4-5: Mick Sharp Photography/Jean Williamson. 5: Mick Sharp
Photography/Mick Sharp. 6: Lesley & Roy Adkins.
7: Michael Holford. 8-9: Mick Sharp Photography/Mick Sharp. 11, 12:
Michael Holford. 13, 15, 17: The Fotomas Index.
18: Mick Sharp Photography. 19, 21(top), 21(bottom),
22: Mary Evans Picture Library. 23: Mary Evans Picture Library/Bruce
Castle Museum. 24-25, 25: Mary Evans Picture Library. 26: The Hulton
Deutsch Collection.
27: The Hulton Getty Picture Collection. 28: Rob Whitrow/Robert Harding
Picture Library.
29: Zefa/Stockmarket.

Artwork
Main illustrators: Mark Bergin, John James, James Field.
Additional illustrations by Bill Donohoe.
Maps by Hayward Art Group.

Cover: Artwork by John James, James Field and
Mark Bergin.

INTRODUCTION

British people have swapped, or traded, goods for thousands of years. At first they simply exchanged their surplus food and other items for goods they needed. Then, during Roman times, Britons began to exchange goods for money instead. But trade would never have grown without transport. All these goods had to be moved. At first, people carried them on foot. Then they used horses, carts and sea-going boats. By Tudor times, merchants were buying goods from countries as far away as India and America. Today, thanks to jet aircraft, huge cargo ships and a rail link with the Continent, Britain trades with all parts of the world.

CONTENTS

THE FIRST TRADERS

The earliest Britons produced nearly all they needed. They hunted for food, or grew it. They built their own houses and made their own tools, pots and clothes. But sometimes they had crops or goods to spare, and exchanged them with their neighbours.

▽ **Maiden Castle in Dorset** was a stronghold built on a hill. It was begun in about 3000 BC. Inside the ramparts was a 'town' of huts. The people who lived here worked the land within an 8 kilometre circle. Others were craftsmen. They probably traded their goods at a regular market held in the hillfort.

▽ **Hillforts were built all over Britain.** England and Wales alone had more than 1,400. The remains of many fort sites can still be seen.

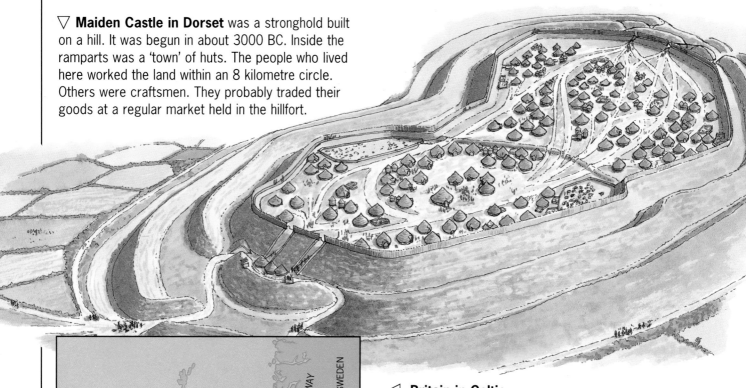

◁ **Britain in Celtic times** (about 200 BC). There were already trade routes from Europe to the south and east coasts.

▷ **Peddars Way in Norfolk,** as it is today. This was a prehistoric trackway that was later improved and used by the Romans. It was part of a long-distance trade route for flint and later for copper and iron, which were used to make axeheads, tools and ornaments.

SCOTLAND

NORWAY

SWEDEN

Trade routes

IRELAND

ENGLAND

WALES

Trade routes

GERMANY

Essex

FLANDERS

Dorset

Kent

GAUL

In about 1000 BC, Britain was a land of hillforts and scattered villages. Inside these small communities, everyone worked together to grow enough food. But a prosperous village might produce a surplus of food. Then some people could spend their time making pots or working metal to make tools.

These were the first specialist craftsmen. They were given food in exchange for their work. Some craftsmen made beautiful objects, such as gold neck rings and iron weapons. Such treasures could be traded with other communities in return for goods which were needed, such as salt or tin.

Trading took place at gatherings like the annual fair at Glastonbury in Somerset. People exchanged such goods as baskets, axes, cloth and coloured glass beads. Trade soon reached overseas. By 100 BC, ships from Gaul (France) were bringing wine, pottery and other goods to the Dorset coast. They carried back British ironwork, corn, cattle and leather.

△ **The Celts,** who settled in Britain in about 500 BC, used pairs of horses to pull their fast war chariots. Bigger carts for carrying heavy loads on farms were pulled by oxen.

▽ **Inside Grime's Graves** in Norfolk, which date from 2600 BC. The black rock is flint, which the miners dug out using picks made of deer antler. Some of the picks can be seen here.

◁ **Crops and other goods** were moved in carts like this farm wagon. The wheels were made of wood.

▷ **The Celts captured prisoners** from other tribes in battle and sold them as slaves to the traders from Europe.

THE ROMANS ARRIVE

"Britain is a most wealthy island," wrote a Roman visitor in about AD 350. The Romans had invaded 400 years before and conquered most of England and Wales. They had been attracted by the natural riches of Britain, especially metals such as tin, lead, gold, silver and iron.

The Romans quickly declared that all metals belonged to them. They started many new mines, including silver mines in Somerset and gold and copper mines in Wales. Iron from Kent was shipped to the Continent.

The Romans brought peace and prosperity. The people who lived in their cities and villas wanted luxury goods, such as wine and fine pottery. At first these had to be imported from Europe. But by AD 200 British craftsmen could make these goods themselves.

▽ **An iron mine in the Weald** (modern Kent). Slaves turn the treadmill which pulls out sledges carrying iron ore. The ore was refined into pure iron at the mine. This made it less bulky to transport.

△ **These large storage pots,** known as amphorae, were made in Gaul and brought to Britain. They were of much better quality than native British pottery.

▷ **The network of roads built by the Romans.** The roads linked the main settlements, from London and Dover in the south to Newstead and Chester in the north. The straight, well-drained roads were made originally for Roman troops to march along. But many merchants also used them, spreading trade to all parts of Britain.

Chester   York
Lincoln
Wroxeter
Dover
Canterbury

△ **Craftsmen** included smiths (above), potters (right), leather-workers and glass-makers.

▷ (Far right) **After about AD 50, London grew into the most important trading centre in Britain.** Huge docks and warehouses were built on either side of the River Thames, and craftsmen set up workshops in the city centre and near the docks. Some of them worked from home.

▷ **A fruit and vegetable stall** in the forum in London.

Goods were carried overland in four-wheeled carts pulled by two or more horses. The drivers travelled on the new Roman roads whenever they could. But although these roads were dry and hard, they were meant for marching men. They went straight up and down hills, which made hard work for the horses.

Transport by water was cheaper. Wooden barges took goods on rivers and early canals, such as Fossdyke near Lincoln. Cargo ships sailed to Europe, or around the coast to Scotland (where they were often attacked by Irish pirates).

△ **The forum**, or centre, of a Roman town. This was an open space where traders ran shops or set up stalls on market days and merchants made business deals. The Romans built many new towns.

▽ **A Roman trader's weighing scales** dating from about AD 50. Lead weights were placed in one pan and the goods to be sold in the other pan. The sliding weight on the bar was used to help the scales balance.

CHANGING TIMES

By AD 300, British trade was booming. The Romans had encouraged people to exchange their goods for bronze or silver coins. For the first time, trade was based on money. As the amount of coinage increased, industries such as pottery and iron-making grew.

▷ **Engineers building a Roman road.** First, they plan the route using a groma, or levelling instrument (left). Then workers clear the ground and lay a base of clay and gravel (centre). More clay and then cobbles are laid on top and along side drainage channels (far right).

There were large pottery factories in Cambridgeshire and Hertfordshire. Farming expanded, too, as the Romans ploughed up new land. So much grain was produced that, in AD 359, loads of it were shipped to feed hungry Roman troops in Gaul.

But Roman power was collapsing. Saxon raiders from Germany and Denmark attacked cargo ships and coastal towns. When the Romans left Britain for good in 410, trade fell apart. No new coins were made, so the supply of money ran out. People went back to the system of 'bartering', or exchanging one kind of goods for another.

The rulers of the new Anglo-Saxon kingdoms encouraged trade once more. They ordered luxury goods, especially gold and silver jewellery, either for themselves or as gifts for other leaders.

▽ **A busy port in late Roman Britain.** Goods are stored in the warehouses along the quay. A flat-bottomed barge with a square sail carries a load of grain and stone upriver. To the right is the stern of a cargo ship. Both boats have large oars at the back to help with steering. The Romans also built lighthouses at ports to guide their ships.

△ **The remains of Wade's Causeway** in North Yorkshire. The top surface of gravel has worn away, but the foundation slabs and stone-lined drains on either side remain. Many modern roads follow the straight routes laid down by Roman engineers.

▽ **A wooden bridge** allows troops and carts to cross easily and safely over a deep river. Roman sentries guard each end. Bridges like this helped traders to carry their goods quickly between towns.

Ports in south-east England, such as Dover, grew quickly. By 550, nearly all trade with France passed through Kent. Here, after 600, the first Anglo-Saxon coins were minted from gold and silver.

As business increased, new ports such as Southampton sprang up in the south. Among the most important exports leaving here for Europe were woollen cloaks, lead and cheese. Imports included Chinese silks, German swords, and wine.

△ **King Alfred** (849-899), here at the front of the main ship, ordered the building of a fleet of big ships, each powered by 60 oars. The ships defended ports against raiders from Scandinavia.

▽ **Angles, Saxons** and other peoples from Northern Germany and Denmark first came to Britain to trade or raid. After the Romans had gone, they invaded.

NEW INVADERS

"Three hundred and fifty ships came to the mouth of the Thames; they ruined Canterbury." Reports like this filled the Anglo-Saxon Chronicle in the years after the first Viking raid in 787. The Vikings plundered food and treasure, shattering British trade once again.

The Vikings swept across the North Sea in their fleets of longships. These boats were ideal for raiding voyages. They were fast and could sail 90 kilometres in a day. They were lightweight and strong so were easy to row with long oars if there was no wind. They had a keel (rib) underneath, which reduced the rolling from side to side.

A longship was about 25 metres long and 2 metres wide. It carried a crew of 40 men with their weapons and food. Even so, there was still room in the sleek hull for plenty of plunder.

▷ **A Viking raiding party** storms ashore. At first, the Vikings merely came to steal and burn. By 850, they were coming to settle.

▽ **Longships took the Vikings** right round Britain and as far as North America and Greenland between AD 800 and 1050.

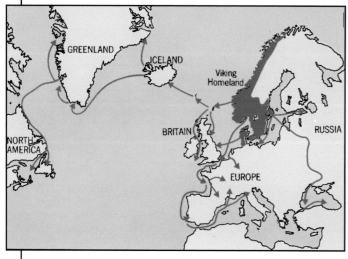

GREENLAND
ICELAND
Viking Homeland
NORTH AMERICA
BRITAIN
RUSSIA
EUROPE

◁ **Coins were stamped** on a silver sheet and then cut out. Anglo-Saxon coins were called *sceattas*, meaning treasure. King Alfred designed special coins to celebrate his victories over the Vikings.

▷ **A hoard of Viking silver** found in Lancashire in 1840. It dates from AD 903.

Not all Vikings were bloodthirsty pirates. Many were farmers looking for new land or traders looking for new markets. Their stout trading ships, known as knarrs, carried goods from Russia and the Baltic Sea in the north and from Spain and the Mediterranean in the south.

By this time, the Vikings had settled in the eastern part of England, in Ireland and in northern Scotland. There were major Viking towns at York, Lincoln, Nottingham and Dublin. Thanks to the trade brought by the Viking sailors, the towns grew very wealthy.

▷ **Market day in a Viking town.**
• A trader has set up his stall, selling wooden buckets and bowls.
• On a leather-worker's stall, shoes and belts are for sale.
• A guard watches from a defensive wall round the town.
• A man has brought a sack of goods to sell.

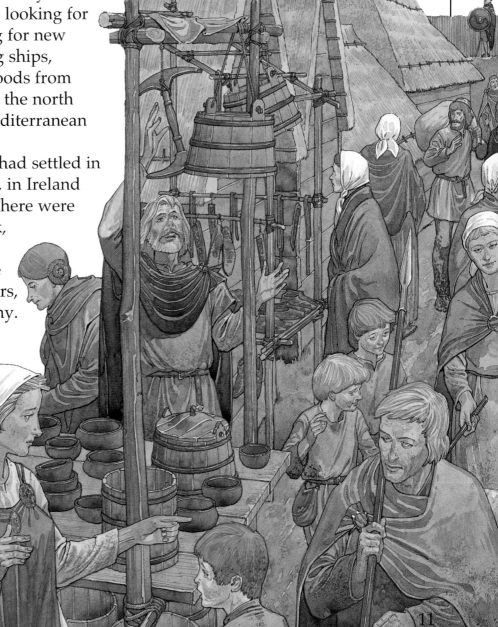

MARKETS AND TAXES

When William of Normandy conquered England, he wanted to find out how much his new kingdom was worth. In 1086 he ordered a survey of every piece of property and who owned it. "There was not even an ox or a cow or a pig left that was not set down in writing", complained one writer.

▷ **A pedlar carrying his goods for sale in a pack on his back** — a carving from a medieval pew (a long seat) from Swaffham Church, Norfolk. By 1400, guilds, or associations of craftsmen, had been set up for many trades. The guilds put many pedlars out of work.

The guilds raised the standard of work of goods and set fixed prices for items on sale.

▽ **Medieval kings** fought many wars, both at home and abroad. In 1096, the wars called the Crusades began in the Middle East. They lasted for 200 years! To pay their armies and for ships, the kings raised money by taxing merchants, tradesmen and landowners. Officers added up the money collected on a squared (chequered) cloth. This was called the Exchequer.

The survey, called Domesday Book, showed that the vast majority of people owned little or nothing. They were peasants who worked on the land and struggled to grow enough food. Money was of little use to them. Stores of grain, meat, cheese and firewood were much more important.

However, they needed some money to pay their taxes to the king's officers. So, if they had food or other produce to spare, they sold it at the nearest market. By about 1250, there was a market within a day's walk of most villages. The biggest markets were held in the local towns. On market day, craftsmen and traders set out their goods. Shoppers could usually buy anything from bread, ale and hot pies to cloth, candles and iron pots.

△ **Fairs were often held in the big cities** on the feast days of saints. They were a time for fun and trade, with jugglers, acrobats, dancing bears and musicians.

By 1300, trade in Britain had changed little since Saxon times. Most workshops and factories were small and made goods for local villages or towns. The main industries were iron-making in the Forest of Dean, lead-mining in Cumbria and woollen clothmaking in southern England. Travel was slow. The only good routes were the old Roman roads. Along the roads came pedlars, who sold their wares to villagers, and men with packhorses carrying goods to ports on the coast.

△ **A medieval tapestry** made in the Netherlands with woollen threads imported from England.

▷ **Increased trade brought a deadly disease** from the Far East, carried by fleas on rats – the plague, or Black Death.

TRADE BEGINS TO GROW

The Black Death struck Britain in 1348. By 1400, this plague had killed about two-fifths of the population. Trade declined in towns and the countryside. But many peasants were actually better off. With fewer mouths to feed, there was more food to go round.

▽ **Merchants** check as their cargo ship is unloaded from a ship in a busy harbour in southern England. Merchants used boys instead of men to carry the loads as they were cheaper to hire. Trading ships brought boxes of spices, silk and dried fruits from the East, casks of wine from France and bales of furs from the Baltic region (Finland and Russia).

▷ **A Tudor port.** Sea ports such as Liverpool and Bristol grew fast in Tudor times. Bristol's success was due to the huge catches of fish made off Newfoundland.

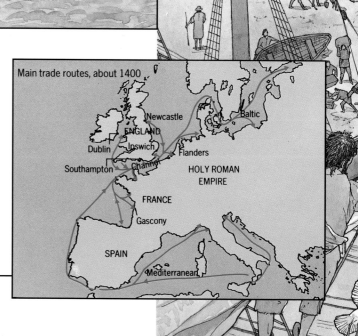

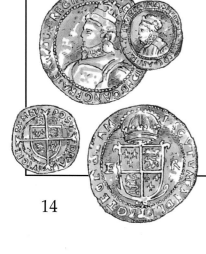

◁ **Tudor coins** were the first to have realistic portraits of kings and queens.

▷ **Trading ships** sailed to and from ports around Britain. Ships from the East, carrying rugs and spices, had to sail round southern and western Africa to reach Britain.

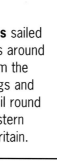

Main trade routes, about 1400

Newcastle
Baltic
ENGLAND
Dublin
Ipswich
Flanders
Southampton
Channel
HOLY ROMAN
EMPIRE
FRANCE
Gascony
SPAIN
Mediterranean

The Black Death also gave a boost to the wool trade. There was a shortage of labourers to plough fields and tend crops. Much farmland was turned into grazing for sheep instead. By 1450, there were less than 3 million people living in England and Wales – and more than 8 million sheep! Sheep's wool had become Britain's most valuable raw material. It was spun into thread, then woven into cloth and exported to Flanders in northern Europe. Many wool merchants became extremely wealthy.

When Henry VII, the first Tudor monarch, took power in 1485, British trade was growing very slowly. London was still the only city as big as the great towns of Europe. Wool was the only major export, and nearly all of it went to a single Dutch port, Antwerp.

But by 1550 things had changed. Antwerp had declined. London had taken most of its trade and become a major centre for buying and selling, and also for lending money to merchants. British ships were carrying a huge variety of goods to Europe – coal, copper, salt, tin and iron as well as cloth.

▷ **Goods being unloaded from a river barge.** Goods landed at ports were transported inland along roads by packhorses or along rivers by small boats and barges like these.

THE WIDE WORLD

In the 1490s, European sailors explored west across the Atlantic. Among them was a Bristol trader, John Cabot. He hoped to reach China and the Far East, where precious silks, jewels and spices could be bought. Instead, he landed on a newly found continent – North America.

▷ **The main exports from the Americas** and some routes taken by Tudor explorers:
1497 John Cabot lands on Newfoundland.
1508 Sebastian Cabot (his son) reaches Hudson Bay.
1576 Martin Frobisher reaches Baffin Island.
1580 Francis Drake ends voyage round the world.
1585 Walter Raleigh tries to set up a colony.

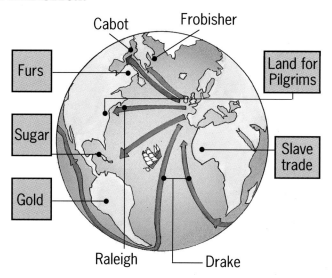

Cabot was disappointed not to reach Asia. But North America had its own riches. There were huge shoals of cod off the coast of Newfoundland. There were animal furs and vast supplies of free timber that could be shipped back to Britain. Later came sugar from the West Indies, tobacco from Virginia, sweetcorn and potatoes. After 1600, settlers from Britain founded colonies on North America's east coast.

Meanwhile, merchants were making stronger links with India, China and the Spice Islands. Some had tried to find a 'North-West Passage' round America to the Far East, but were blocked by ice. Others formed trading companies to buy goods from India, Ceylon (Sri Lanka), Turkey and the eastern Mediterranean.

▽ **Following Christopher Columbus's discovery of America in 1492,** Spain and Portugal drew up a treaty claiming different parts of South America as theirs. The Spanish barred British traders from their colonies. This led to the battle of the Spanish Armada of 1588.

△ **Francis Drake and his soldiers attack Cartagena,** a Spanish trading post in present-day Colombia, South America. Spanish ships carried gold and silver from America to Europe. British sailors such as Drake attacked these fleets and stole the treasure.

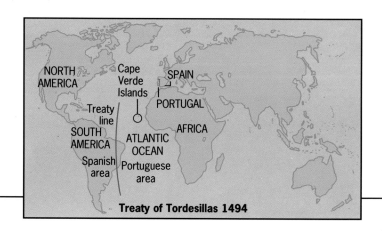

Treaty of Tordesillas 1494

△ **Sailors on long voyages** rarely had fresh food.

▷ **The *Sovereign of the Seas,*** Britain's biggest warship, was built in 1637.

◁ **Slave traders and soldiers** attack a village in South America, killing the villagers and looting their treasure. They shipped the treasure to Europe to sell. Slave dealers grew very rich from the 'triangular' (three-sided) trade:

• British traders sailed from Bristol and Liverpool to West Africa with cloth and guns.
• They traded these with European merchants for black African slaves.
• The slaves were taken to the West Indies.
• On the islands, they were traded for a cargo of sugar or gold.
• The sugar or gold was carried back to England and sold at a large profit.

By 1700, Britain was one of the richest nations in the world. A huge fleet of merchant ships brought goods from all over the world, including Russia, France, India, Morocco and North America. Britain also controlled the valuable sugar industry. Most important of all, Britain controlled the sea. The powerful Spanish and Dutch fleets had been defeated, and British sailors had few other rivals.

MILLS AND MARKETS

Until the 1700s, most goods were made by hand. One of the most important goods was cotton cloth. In their homes, workers spun the cotton into thread. Others wove the thread into cloth. This was a slow process that could not keep up with the booming demand.

Ways had to be found to speed up production. The answer lay in machines that could do the work of several people, and in putting workers together in factories. During the Georgian period (1714 to 1837), spinning and weaving machines, steam engines and improved iron-smelting methods were invented and industrial towns grew.

This was the start of what we call the Industrial Revolution. Goods were now produced cheaply, quickly and in huge quantities. Surplus goods were exported (sold abroad), so overseas trade grew rapidly. Trade in Britain also grew as factory workers had money to spend.

▽ **Ironbridge in Telford, Shropshire.** Built in 1779, it was the world's first iron bridge. New bridges made it easier to carry raw materials to factories and finished goods to large towns to be sold in shops.

▷ **The centre of the new pottery industry** was in the English Midlands. But it depended greatly on improved forms of transport. Cargo ships and canal boats brought clay from Cornwall and coal from the North.

▽ **Mill owners liked to employ women and children** because they could pay them less than men. Workers operated machines that could spin many threads at once and weave wide lengths of cloth. Rows of machines were set up in large mills (left).

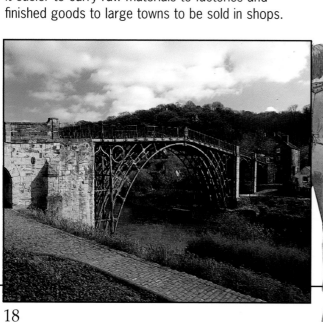

◁ **Trials of an early steam locomotive in 1808.**The first steam locomotives were used to carry coal from mines to ports and iron foundries.

▽ **'Narrow boats'** carried coal, clay and many other goods along specially dug canals. The boats were pulled by horses or, later, powered by steam engines.

THE TIGER

BUSY BRITAIN

"First one passes a watch-maker's, then a silk or fan store, now a silversmith's, a china or glass shop." This is how a German visitor described London's Oxford Street in 1786. The bustling street contained over 150 shops, which stayed open until 10 o'clock at night.

Never before had British shops had such a variety of things to sell. Many of these goods were imported from overseas. People could buy spices from Sri Lanka, silks and delicate pottery from China, tea from India and coffee and chocolate from Central America.

But imports had to be paid for. This wealth was produced by the growing trade in exported raw materials. Scotland exported meat, salt and flax threads to make linen. England exported building stone, wheat and coal.

Meanwhile, British industry was expanding fast. Factories and foundries turned raw materials into finished goods. Cotton fibres from North America were woven into cloth. Sugar cane and tobacco from the West Indies were refined, and iron ore was cast and hammered.

△ **'Blackbeard'**, one of the ruthless pirates who attacked cargo ships sailing between North America and Europe. Pirates brought terror to every important trade route and became rich on the illegal sale of the stolen goods. But as Britain's Royal Navy grew stronger in the early 1700s, pirates were hunted down.

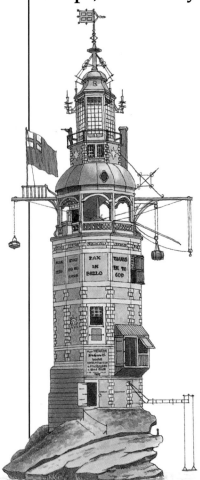

△ **The first Eddystone lighthouse** (1698) warned sailors of dangerous rocks off the Cornish coast. The number of cargo ships grew swiftly during the 18th century – and so did the need for lighthouses to guide them. The first oil light, reflected from mirrors, was built in 1763.

▷ **A toll gate at Kensington in London.** Ordinary roads were often muddy and full of holes but turnpike roads were well-kept. Carriages could travel faster on turnpikes, but a toll, or fee, had to be paid to use them.

▽ **Cities grew fast in Georgian times** as increasing trade brought in more money. Grand new streets and city centres were built in London, Edinburgh, Bristol, Glasgow and Manchester. Shops became grander, too, with big plate-glass windows and smart display stands for the goods. Some shopping streets were lit with oil lamps for the first time, to discourage thieves. But there was still room for poorer traders, such as the flower girl, the fruitseller, the street fiddler and the pedlar shown here.

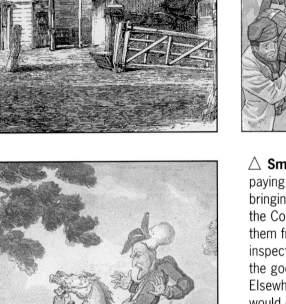

△ **Smugglers** avoided paying taxes by secretly bringing in goods from the Continent and hiding them from the tax inspectors. They sold the goods in the towns. Elsewhere, poachers would catch fish or game animals, such as rabbits and pheasants, from landowners' estates to feed their families.

◁ **Highwaymen** hold up a traveller at gunpoint to steal his money and valuables, such as rings and watches. Most criminals were never caught.

For many years, most British goods had been sold in Europe. But as the Empire grew, trade increased with North America, the West Indies and India. This meant that British traders were buying cheap raw materials from the colonies and then selling them back as expensive finished goods! Between 1700 and 1790, Britain's foreign trade doubled and exports rose dramatically.

THE AGE OF STEAM

In 1804, Richard Trevithick built the first steam engine light enough to move itself along iron rails. In 1819, a steamship crossed the Atlantic for the first time. Steam power was about to become the driving force behind Britain's rapid growth in trade.

▷ **The development of steam-powered transport**, by railway or steamship, made travel between colonies in the Empire much quicker and safer. By 1899, the British Empire stretched all round the world.

▷ (Far right) **Three forms of steam transport** at a busy port in the 1880s – train, paddle-steamer and traction engine.

▽ **The industrial landscape of Wolverhampton,** in the Midlands of England, in 1866.

Canada
Bahamas
Jamaica
Sierra Leone
Gambia
Gold Coast
Nigeria
British Guiana
Egypt
Sudan
Aden
British East Africa
India
Burma
Ceylon
Singapore
Hong Kong
British New Guinea
South Africa
Australia
New Zealand

Countries under British control are marked in red

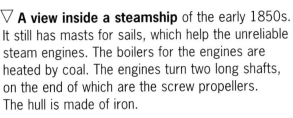
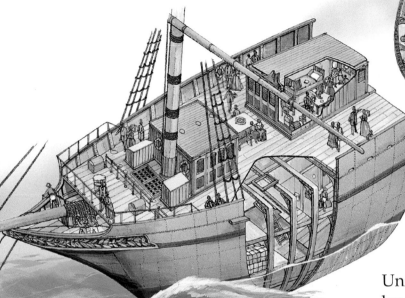

▽ **A view inside a steamship** of the early 1850s. It still has masts for sails, which help the unreliable steam engines. The boilers for the engines are heated by coal. The engines turn two long shafts, on the end of which are the screw propellers. The hull is made of iron.

Until Victorian times, goods were moved by muscle power or wind power. The muscles of horses pulled carts or barges. The wind blew sailing ships. But animals got tired and the wind often stopped blowing. The invention of the steam engine brought a stronger kind of power. These engines were never tired and took no notice of the weather. And one steam engine could do the work of 100 horses.

The world's first public steam-powered railway was built in 1825 to carry coal from Darlington to the port of Stockton. By the late 1830s, there were rail links between many major towns. By 1840, steamships were making regular voyages across the Atlantic Ocean.

Steam power had a huge impact on trade and industry. It drove spinning and weaving machines in cotton mills. It powered bellows for blast furnaces, and hammers in iron foundries. It could even be used to pull ploughs and thresh corn.

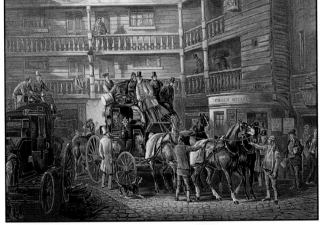

△ **A stagecoach** prepares to set off on a journey. People continued to travel by horse-drawn vehicles well after the railway system was developed.

▷ **The tall 'penny-farthing'** and a tricycle, early bicycles.

TRAVELLING BY TRAIN

"The sensation of flying was quite delightful", wrote actress Fanny Kemble in 1830. She had not been in an aircraft, of course, but a train. Though the early trains reached a speed of only about 30 kilometres an hour, it must have seemed like flying!

At this time, the fastest form of travel was on a galloping horse. Trains were stronger, and were to become faster than horses. The first train to run on the Stockton & Darlington Railway in 1825 carried nearly 600 people. By 1900, more than 1,000 million journeys were made by train each year.

The railways also carried vast amounts of goods, from fresh milk to china clay. The most important cargo was coal, going from the mines of Wales and northern England to factories, iron foundries and gas works.

△ **Inside a station** of London's underground steam-railway system, which was started in 1863. On its first day, the 'Metropolitan Railway' carried 30,000 passengers – in open carriages behind the steam locomotive. The single line ran from Paddington station to Farringdon in the City.

▽ **A locomotive on the Great Western Railway** is prepared for a day's work in the 1870s. Railwaymen were proud of their engines and kept the brass and paintwork clean and polished. Coal for the boiler was carried in the tender (truck) at the rear.

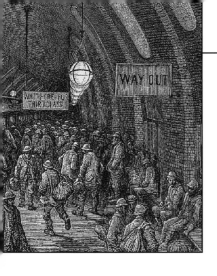

▷ **A passenger steam train** pulls into a country station in the 1880s. The station master checks that the train is on time. By now, travelling by rail had become faster, cheaper, more convenient and safer than travelling by road.

Railways changed the appearance of the landscape. Tunnels and cuttings were dug. Bridges carried trains over valleys and rivers. New lines cut across towns on their way to new stations. Trains also changed the way many people lived. City workers could travel to their offices from homes far away. And people could afford holiday trips to the seaside.

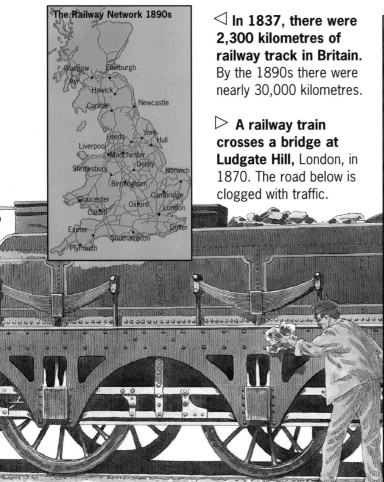

The Railway Network 1890s

◁ **In 1837, there were 2,300 kilometres of railway track in Britain.** By the 1890s there were nearly 30,000 kilometres.

▷ **A railway train crosses a bridge at Ludgate Hill,** London, in 1870. The road below is clogged with traffic.

BY LAND, SEA AND AIR

As the 20th century began, Britain's trade seemed as strong as ever. British cloth, steel, coal and ships were being sold all over the world. At the same time, new kinds of transport were appearing, which could carry people and goods farther, faster and more efficiently.

▽ **The *Queen Mary*,** launched in 1934, was a famous luxury liner. During the Second World War (1939-45), she was used to carry troops – 15,000 at a time!

▷ **At work on a car-production line** at Cowley, near Oxford, in 1930. At this time, many different kinds of vehicles (old and new) were being used above and below the streets. They included:
- horsedrawn carts
- motor cars, vans and lorries
- steam lorries
- motor buses
- tramcars, powered by electricity
- underground trains, also electric.

Steam was still the major form of power on railways and farms. Steamships could now travel at greater speeds, thanks to the development of the turbine engine in 1884. By 1910, British ships were carrying half of the world's cargoes.

But steam was soon giving way to a new invention – the petrol engine. In 1914, there were already 130,000 motor cars and lorries on the roads. After the First World War (1914-1918), this total rose rapidly. Petrol engines also powered the first aircraft. The earliest planes could fly only short distances with two or three passengers. After 1918, better engines meant that bigger aircraft could be built.

▷ **Airline passengers** arrive at London's first big airport at Croydon, which opened in 1920. By this time, more than 65,000 British people were travelling by air each year (although tickets were expensive, and only wealthy people or businessmen could afford them). There were regular flights to Paris, Brussels and Amsterdam. In 1924, the new Imperial Airways brought air links with countries of the British Empire, including South Africa and India.

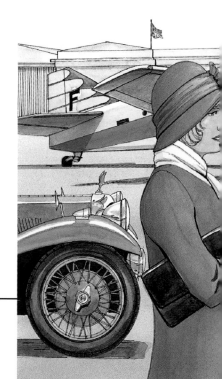

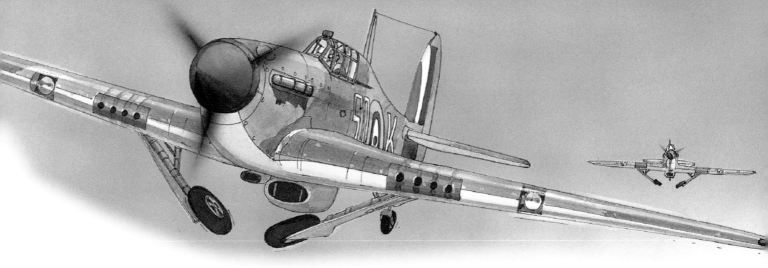

△ **The *Mallard*,** the fastest ever steam-locomotive in 1938.

△ **During the Second World War,** Britain was saved from invasion by the deeds of its RAF pilots, flying fighter aircraft such as the Hurricanes (above) and Spitfires. The Spitfire had been developed from an earlier British seaplane financed by private money.

◁ **Air passengers** board a new jet airliner in 1952. International travel was growing rapidly. Now the Atlantic could be crossed in 8 hours.

By 1950, many of Britain's old industries, such as textiles and shipbuilding, were in decline. This was partly because of the damage brought by the two World Wars. But it also showed that other trading nations were making goods more cheaply than Britain. Textiles were being made in India and the Far East, and iron and steel in Germany, Russia and the USA.

Many people were thrown out of work as factories and mines closed down. But after the Second World War, new industries, such as chemicals, electronics and car making, began to create new jobs. Many new, up-to-date, factories were built.

THE MODERN AGE

Despite its new industries, Britain's trade still declined after 1950. In 1982, more money was spent on importing manufactured goods than exporting them. This had never happened before. One newspaper said "the great Victorian engine of prosperity had finally run out of steam".

Competition from developing countries, especially in the Far East, grew quickly. The British Empire was broken up and many of the old colonies began to look for new markets for their goods. Most, however, formed a new group of countries (including Britain) called the Commonwealth, which promised to trade with each other.

As it had done before the Stuart period, Britain was selling more of its goods in Europe. In 1973 it joined the six countries in the European Economic Community (EEC), or Common Market. EEC members aimed to make it cheaper to buy each other's products.

▷ **A modern out-of-town shopping area.** In recent years, shopping has become big business. Many shops and supermarkets have grown in size and have moved from the 'high street' in town centres to huge shopping malls, or complexes, outside. People usually drive to these shopping areas or park nearby and take shuttle buses to and from the shops. Shops that have remained in towns have had to stay open longer hours to compete.

▷ **A new tram runs on tracks** alongside a roadway in Manchester. With ever-increasing volumes of cars and lorries on roads, many cities have built new railways and tram systems to encourage people to use public transport instead. They have also introduced special lanes on roads for buses or bicycles to allow 'environmentally friendly' forms of transport to move faster.

All the same, in the late-1990s many British people have more money to spend than ever before. They spend it on their houses, on foreign holidays, on leisure activities and on consumer goods – many of which are imported. Nowadays, nearly 90 per cent of all households own a television, a washing machine and a telephone.

People also travel long distances more regularly. Most families own at least one car (by 1995 there were 20 million cars on the roads). The journey to Europe is now easier with the opening of the Channel Tunnel between England and France, and high-speed trains and jet aircraft can cross from country to country in a few hours.

▷ **The trading floor of a financial company in London.** Around 1900, nearly three-quarters of working people worked in factories, mines or on farms, actually making things. Today, most people work in shops and offices. 'Service industries', such as insurance and banking, are now Britain's greatest exports. The City of London is one of most important financial centres in the world.

Places to Visit

Here are some sites relating to trade and transport in Britain. Your local Tourist Office will be able to tell you about other places in your area.

Bo'Ness & Kineeil Railway, West Lothian. Scotland's biggest collection of steam locomotives.

Darlington Railway Centre, Cleveland. Exhibits include *Locomotion I*, the engine that opened the Stockton & Darlington Railway.

Didcot Railway Centre, Oxfordshire. Includes a reconstruction of the original Broad Gauge track.

Dock Museum, Barrow-in-Furness. Shows how steel ships were built in Victorian times.

Dolaucothi Roman Gold Mines, Dyfed. Guided tours of mines that are more than 1,500 years old.

Duxford Airfield, Cambridgeshire. A huge collection of famous aircraft, old and new.

Glasgow Museum of Transport, Glasgow. All kinds of vehicles, from fire engines to double-deck buses.

Maritime and Industrial Museum, Swansea. Exhibits showing life on the dockside and in a woollen mill.

National Motor Museum, Beaulieu, Hampshire. More than 250 vehicles showing how cars have developed.

National Railway Museum, York. Everything from Stephenson's *Rocket* (a replica) to *Le Shuttle*.

SS Great Britain, Bristol. One of the greatest Victorian steamships, now being fully restored.

Severn Bridges, Gloucestershire and South Wales. Two of the longest suspension bridges in the world, side-by-side.

Ulster Folk and Transport Museum, County Down. Exhibits include donkey carts, schooners, steam railways and aircraft.

Further Reading

Here are some books that will tell you more about the topics covered here.

A Sense of History series by Sallie Purkis, Longman 1994-1996 – books, activity cards, teachers' packs.

Heritage series, Wayland 1997

History of Britain: Victorian Railways by Andrew Langley, Heinemann, 1996

History of Britain: Victorian Steamships by Andrew Langley, Heinemann, 1997.

History of Fairs and Markets by Richard Wood, Wayland 1996.

Then and Now: Farming, Transport, Franklin Watts, 1997.

GLOSSARY

barter To exchange or trade goods without using money.

colony A permanent settlement founded overseas by a country.

export To sell goods to another country.

foundry A factory where metal is purified and cast into shapes.

guild An association of traders or craftsmen.

import To buy goods from another country.

liner A ship which carries passengers on a regular route.

merchant A person who makes their living by buying and selling things, either in their own country or abroad.

peasant A farmer or labourer who works on the land.

pedlar A tradesman on foot, who sells goods in the street or from door to door.

shuttle In weaving, a device that carries the horizontal thread back and forth between the vertical threads.

specialist A worker who devotes himself or herself to one craft or trade.

Spice Islands Islands in the Far East where spices were grown (now the Moluccas).

spices Plants such as pepper, cinnamon and ginger, used to flavour foods.

surplus More than is needed.

tax A sum of money or goods demanded by a government to pay for services.

traction engine A steam-powered vehicle that pulled heavy goods on roads.

treadmill A mill wheel turned by people or animals walking on steps inside.

warehouse A large building for storing goods.

watermill A mill wheel turned by the force of running water.

TIMECHART

3000 BC Early markets held in hillforts.

AD 43 Romans invade.

410 Romans withdraw.

787 First Viking raid.

1066 Normans conquer.

1086 William I orders Domesday survey.

1348 Black Death.

1497 Cabot lands in North America.

1600 East India Company formed.

1607 First colony set up in America. Its settlers sell tobacco to English traders.

1759 The first canal built.

1804 Trevithick's first steam locomotive.

1825 Stockton & Darlington Railway opens.

1837 Steamship *Great Western* crosses the Atlantic.

1896 Cars first allowed on British roads.

1920 First airport opened at Croydon.

1958 First motorway, the M1, opened.

1995 Channel Tunnel opened.

INDEX